HOW TO
BE A
Lady

OTHER GENTLEMANNERS™ BOOKS

How to Be a Gentleman
John Bridges

A Gentleman Entertains
John Bridges and Bryan Curtis

As a Gentleman Would Say
John Bridges and Bryan Curtis

A Gentleman Gets Dressed Up
John Bridges and Bryan Curtis

A Gentleman Walks Down the Aisle
John Bridges and Bryan Curtis

Toasts and Tributes
John Bridges and Bryan Curtis

50 Things Every Young Gentleman Should Know
Kay West with John Bridges and Bryan Curtis

50 Things Every Young Lady Should Know
Kay West with John Bridges and Bryan Curtis

As a Lady Would Say
Sheryl Shade

How to Raise a Gentleman
Kay West

How to Raise a Lady
Kay West

A Lady at the Table
Sheryl Shade with John Bridges

A Gentleman at the Table
John Bridges and Bryan Curtis

A Gentleman Abroad
John Bridges and Bryan Curtis

HOW TO

BE A

Lady

REVISED AND EXPANDED

....

A CONTEMPORARY GUIDE
TO COMMON COURTESY

CANDACE SIMPSON-GILES

THOMAS NELSON
Since 1798

NASHVILLE   DALLAS   MEXICO CITY   RIO DE JANEIRO

Published in Nashville, Tennessee, by Thomas Nelson. Thomas Nelson is a registered trademark of Thomas Nelson, Inc.

Thomas Nelson, Inc., titles may be purchased in bulk for educational, business, fund-raising, or sales promotional use. For information, please e-mail SpecialMarkets@ThomasNelson.com.

ISBN: 978-1-4016-0459-2

The Library of Congress has cataloged an earlier edition of this book as follows:

Simpson-Giles, Candace, 1953–
  How to be a lady / by Candace Simpson-Giles.
     p. cm.
  ISBN: 978-1-5585-3939-6
  1. Etiquette for women. I. Title.
  BJ1856 .S56 2001
  395.1'44—dc21
2001004337

Printed in the United States of America

12 13 14 15 16 WOR 6 5 4 3

To my mother, Margie Smith, who taught me that being a lady was one of the most important parts of being a woman

CONTENTS

INTRODUCTION

*W*hen *How to Be a Lady* was first published in 2001, the world was a vastly different place. The emergence of the Internet as how we communicate, shop, and meet new people has definitely been a game changer in the world of etiquette as we know it. In today's world we do most of our communicating on cell phones and computers. Going through security at the airport is much more complicated than it was ten years ago. But despite how different things are, the principles of good manners remain the same. "Please" and "Thank you" still work on almost every occasion. And treating others the way you want to be treated is still the way a lady should conduct her life. So despite the new pressures women today feel because of our changing world, it is important to maintain the patience and civility that every lady has.

Being a woman does not automatically make one a lady. The term *lady* has evolved to mean many new and different things over the past 100 years. Manners, attitudes, appropriate dress, and social mores have changed so dramatically that our grandmother's definition of being a lady hardly resembles today's expectations.

The rapid evolution of the modern woman over the last century has brought with it both confusion and fulfillment. Women have stepped back and asked themselves just exactly how to properly handle their new status and situations that arise in their professional careers and active personal lives. White gloves and hats are not as much a part of our dress standard as they were for the women of earlier generations, nor does a woman find that she has to have a male escort to attend functions.

A lady by today's definition knows that educating herself in every way possible, from higher education to common sense manners, empowers her to become a woman of accomplishment and poise. She knows that it is not the dress size she wears or the money she possesses that brings her satisfaction in life. A lady knows that beauty and wealth can be fleeting, but her inner character is the measure by which others will ultimately judge her as a person. Her courtesies, the high esteem in which she holds herself and others, and her sincere words of praise and thoughtfulness will reflect her strong values and place her ahead in the minds and hearts of those who know her. Being thought of as a "lady" may be one of the highest compliments a woman can receive in life.

Chapter One

A LADY EXPERIENCES REAL LIFE

A lady is always on her toes; she
realizes that every encounter makes
lasting impressions.

～

A lady knows how to make
others feel at ease.

～

A lady is gracious and thankful for
any gesture of common courtesy
directed toward her.

～

When a lady is asked to be a bridesmaid,
she accepts the request as an honor. If she
does not particularly like the dress, she
keeps this to herself.

A lady does not use her camera phone in ways that intrude upon the privacy of others.

~

A lady understands that if the taking of photographs is prohibited at any concert or other performances or in an art gallery that also means camera-phone pictures or videos.

~

A lady doesn't ask dating couples when they are getting married. Likewise, she doesn't ask married couples when or if they are planning to have children.

~

A lady never compliments one person when she is in a group setting. She chooses a moment when the two of them are alone to offer her compliment.

A lady knows how to prioritize her life in order to make herself available to family, friends, career, and other important considerations in her life. She also knows when she is feeling stretched too thin and how to pull back and sort out her priorities.

⌒

A lady respects other people's time whether at the office or at home.

A Lady and Her Cell Phone

Although a cell phone is probably the most visible and commonplace tool for communication in today's world, a lady does her best to use her cell phone in the most unobtrusive manner possible. She knows that, while a cell phone may be a necessity, there is no reason she should forget she is a lady when using one. A lady is very careful not to place greater importance on the person on the other end of her telephone conversation than the people in her immediate company. That means that, if she is on the telephone when she pulls up at the dry cleaners, she finishes her conversation in the car and does not attempt to conduct her transaction and carry on a conversation at the same time. That also means that, unless there is an extreme emergency, a lady does not interrupt a personal conversation over lunch to take a phone call.

A lady's telephone conversations, whether business or private, are still personal. She knows that others in her immediate vicinity do not want to hear her close a deal or recount the details of a television show. A lady knows that other people are no more interested in hearing her private conversations than she is in hearing theirs.

If a lady must make or receive a phone call while she is in a public place, she moves to a spot where she will cause the least possible disturbance.

A lady never asks friends who are professionals, such as lawyers or doctors, for free advice in their area of specialty. She makes an appointment to see them at their office and fully expects to pay for the services they provide. Should the friends offer their services for free or for a reduced cost, she accepts their gesture graciously.

A Lady Goes to the Theater

Whether attending the theater on a date or with friends, a lady makes every possible effort to be on time for the performance. Not doing so shows a lack of respect for both the performers and fellow audience members.

If she should arrive late, a lady follows the instructions of the ushers. She realizes her tardiness may result in waiting to be seated during a break in the performance. When that break arrives, she goes to her seat as quickly and quietly as possible.

Because a lady is considerate of others around her, she does not talk during the performance. Likewise, if she must bring her cell phone with her, she turns it off before entering the theater. A well-prepared lady has a cough drop in her purse, whether for herself or the person with whom she attends the performance and, when allowed, a bottle of water. If a lady finds herself surprised by an uncontrollable coughing jag, she leaves the theater both for her own good and for the good of others.

A lady is prepared when she walks up to an ATM machine or is in the drive-thru lane at a bank. If she isn't prepared, she offers to let the person in line behind her go first while she fills out her deposit slip.

～

If a lady finds herself in the company of someone who is embarrassing her, she may ask to be taken home. Should her friend refuse, a lady may feel free to leave, even if that means calling a cab or asking another friend for a ride home.

～

A lady holds her temper when dealing with customer service representatives on the phone, no matter how indifferent they may seem or what their language may be. She knows that arguing with an anonymous person on the other end of a telephone line will get her nowhere.

～

If a lady must excuse herself from the dinner table, she simply says, "Excuse me." No further explanation is necessary.

At the laundromat, a lady never takes another person's laundry out of the washer or the dryer, no matter how long she has been waiting. If she is in a hurry, she asks for the attendant's assistance. If there is no attendant, she chooses another laundromat.

～

A lady returns any item she borrows in a timely manner and in the same condition she received it, and if appropriate, a note of thanks is a nice gesture.

～

A lady never makes a date out of desperation.

～

A lady does not discuss her personal relationship breakups with others.

～

A lady never gives the impression she is on the rebound.

A lady never points out the imperfections of her mate to others.

⌒

A lady is very careful about criticizing the mate of anyone, even if she is asked her opinion.

⌒

A lady does not judge others when she learns that a couple has met on an online dating site or in any other manner that might not be her personal cup of tea.

⌒

When walking her dog, a lady always cleans up after her pet.

⌒

A lady treats all animals and pets with the same respect she gives human beings.

⌒

A lady learns how she looks best when being photographed.

A Lady Attends a Funeral

A lady recognizes that a funeral is a time for paying her respects. She wears a conservative dark suit or dress. If there is a wake, a reception, or a visitation with the deceased's family, she arrives on time and waits quietly in the receiving line. She keeps her remarks simple and sincere with words such as "I am so sorry for the loss of your son. He was a good friend to me and I will miss him and his wonderful spirit."

Conversation with others during the service should be limited, and a lady sits where the ushers (if there are any) instruct her. A lady always signs the guest book.

A lady may attend the funeral or service of anyone she has known personally or professionally, at least if they have been on speaking terms. If the deceased person has shown her a particular kindness—especially if she has ever been entertained in the deceased person's home—a lady makes a point to show her respect.

A lady leaves her cell phone in her purse, if at all possible, when she is enjoying a night out on the town.

⌒

A lady always turns off her cell phone when she is attending any type of performance, religious service, or business meeting. If she is on call or expecting an important call, she puts her phone on vibrate.

⌒

Despite the temptation to share, a lady does not text, tweet, Facebook, or send e-mails while she is in the company of others.

⌒

A lady never points out another's bad manners.

⌒

If a lady arrives late for a performance of any type, she waits until there is an appropriate pause and then very quietly slips into her seat.

If a lady arrives late for a church service or a funeral, she waits until there is an appropriate pause and then very quietly slips into the first available seat in the back of the sanctuary.

~

A lady makes every effort not to be late.

~

A lady stays away from public gatherings (and even work) if she feels that she is contagious or has a fever.

A Lady Goes Through a Checkout Line

A lady is prone to run into many friends and acquaintances on her trips to the grocery store. And while she gladly listens to stories about friends' vacations and newborn babies in front of the fresh pasta (as long as she is not blocking the accessibility of others), once a lady arrives at the checkout line, she is all business.

A lady does not needlessly hold up the checkout line. At the register she has her method of payment ready with coupons in hand. She never goes through the express line when she has too many items. If another shopper engages her in conversation, a lady does not hold up those waiting behind her or the cashier. A lady knows that it is her job to make the checkout lines of life move along.

Whenever possible, a lady excuses herself when she has a sneezing attack or a profusely runny nose.

~

A lady does not talk during a performance, a sermon, or a lecture.

~

If a lady must talk to someone during a movie, she does so in the quietest whisper possible, so that she does not disturb those around her.

~

If a lady arrives at a door first, she opens it for the person entering behind her.

~

A lady always says thank you to anyone that holds a door open for her, even if she in in the middle of a conversation with someone she is walking with or on the telephone. A lady is never too busy to acknowledge kindnesses that are shown her.

A lady should always be a good neighbor and offer help when she sees it is needed.

⌒

At a concert or any other musical performance, a lady does not applaud until the end of a complete musical number. If she is unsure, she follows the lead of others in the audience.

⌒

If a lady has left a message for another person—be it on the phone or via e-mail—she does not leave badgering follow-up calls, especially if no deadline is involved.

A lady knows that the gym is her opportunity to get in shape. She should be focused on her workout and dressed appropriately so she is not a distraction to others or even to herself as she jogs or does aerobic movements. A lady is careful to wear clothes that support her bust line and wears tights or shorts that are complimentary to her figure and functional at the same time. She doesn't use the gym for getting dates or catching up on the latest gossip. A lady knows that if she is serious at the gym, it will pay off.

A Lady Takes an Airplane Flight

Almost invariably, the passengers on an airplane have been brought together by a mix of chance and necessity. A lady understands that, in such situations, it is important for everyone to abide by the rules.

In today's world, a lady knows that she must arrive at the airport in plenty of time to get her boarding pass, check her luggage, and pass through airport security without having to rush to her gate. A lady is organized when she reaches the security scanners and removes her shoes, jewelry, and whatever articles of clothing that are required in order to ensure that other travellers are not held up. A lady is pleasant when dealing with security personnel regardless of how unpleasant this activity is for both of them. She brings on board only the amount of luggage that is permitted. She is careful when she stows it overhead to prevent injury to her fellow passengers and to herself. If a bag or parcel is small enough, she stows it under the seat in front of her. She does not intrude on space that is allotted for another passenger's use. She sits in the seat that is assigned to her. If she has sat in the wrong seat and is asked to move, she does not argue about it.

She gets up and finds the place to which she has been assigned. On the other hand, she feels no obligation to give up her rightful seat to another person.

If it is at all possible, a lady stays in her seat throughout the entire flight. A trip to the restroom is almost the only excuse to do otherwise. On extremely long flights a lady does not hesitate to leave her seat for a short time to stretch her legs. When she must leave her seat, a lady excuses herself as unobtrusively as possible, making sure not to step on other passengers' feet.

An airplane flight is one of the few instances in life when it is entirely appropriate for two people to be together for several hours and never speak at all. They may begin the flight as strangers and end it the same way, without anyone having reason to feel neglected or insulted.

A lady graciously accepts a compliment. She does not downgrade herself as if she did not deserve the admiration from the other person or persons. She simply responds with, "Thank you."

⌒

A lady never eats her lunch while she is behind the wheel of a car.

⌒

A lady does not text and drive at the same time.

⌒

If a lady cannot conduct a phone conversation and drive at the same time, she does not try to do so. If she must make or take a call, she pulls over so that she can give her full attention to the matter at hand.

⌒

If a lady is in a state where it is against the law to talk on your cell phone while driving, she does not talk on her cell phone while driving.

A LADY EXPERIENCES REAL LIFE

A lady knows how to behave in other people's churches. If the congregation stands, she stands. She does not, however, need to cross herself, bow, or kneel.

~

A lady does not use her car horn indiscriminately. On the other hand, she is not sheepish about giving an occasional honk to avert disaster.

~

A lady uses her turn signals.

~

A lady does not put her makeup on while driving a car.

~

A lady parks her car carefully. She does not bang her car door into the vehicle next to her. If she scratches another car, she leaves a note.

A lady does not telephone someone
at a terribly early or extremely late
hour unless it is an emergency.
She is also careful to try to avoid
making calls to a person during
what may be a dinner hour.

~

A lady who lives in a condominium
or an apartment is mindful of her
neighbors and keeps the volume of her
television set and stereo at a level she
knows will not disturb others.

~

A lady never takes her pets to
other people's homes, unless she is
specifically urged to do so.
A lady does not feel obligated to invite
other people's pets to her home.

~

A lady doesn't encourage
another person's dog to bark
nor does she tease it.

A lady does not touch other people's children unless she is invited to do so. Neither does she overexcite them.

⌒

If a bellhop offers to assist a lady in hailing a cab, a lady may accept the offer, but understands that a tip is implied.

⌒

When a lady recognizes friends and acquaintances at other tables in a restaurant, she feels free to greet them, but only in the least intrusive way possible. She may stop by their table to greet them cordially, but she does not interrupt their dinner or their conversation for long.

⌒

When a lady makes her way down a row in a crowded theater, she faces the people who are already in their seats. A lady never forces others to stare at her backside.

A lady always says something nice about someone or just doesn't speak of him or her at all. A lady lets people form their own opinions of others.

⌒

A lady doesn't kiss and tell.

⌒

When a lady agrees to be a bridesmaid, she understands that she will be asked to pitch in on some gifts.

⌒

When a bride tells a lady that she can wear her bridesmaid dress again, she nods and smiles.

⌒

A lady is quick to compliment the good manners of another lady's children. When a lady is in the presence of a sneezing person, she offers a quick "Bless you" or, at the very least, a secular but caring "Gesundheit!"

If a lady lives in an upstairs apartment or condominium, she remembers that high heels make a ghastly chatter upon hardwood floors.

~

When a lady vacates a house or apartment where she has been living, she leaves it clean.

Chapter Two

A LADY GETS DRESSED

When a lady is unsure of how to dress for a particular occasion, she asks her host.

A lady does not wear clothes so revealing that they embarrass others.

A lady does not wear clothing so tight or revealing she embarrasses herself. A lady wears clothing that is complimentary to her age and weight.

A lady thinks about who will be attending an event before she chooses her wardrobe.

A lady knows what colors, fabrics, and patterns flatter her.

⌒

Likewise, a lady knows what colors, fabrics, and patterns do nothing for her and she avoids them unless it is in a bridesmaid dress she is being forced to wear.

⌒

When a lady chooses a bridesmaid dress, she remembers all of the horrible dresses she has seen and been made to wear and chooses one that will be flattering to all of her attendants.

⌒

A lady has her heels resoled and the taps replaced when needed.

⌒

A lady thinks twice about wearing a pair of shoes with extremely high heels if she is going to have to do a lot of walking or be on her feet for a long period of time.

A lady makes sure her shoes are appropriately polished.

～

A lady knows what color shoes to wear with her outfit.

～

A lady does not wear shoes that clash with the rest of her outfit.

～

A lady wears a camisole if her blouse or dress is sheer enough to reveal the details of her bra.

～

A lady builds her wardrobe on a foundation of well-made clothes that will not be out of style after one season and will endure repeated cleaning and wear.

A Lady and Her Purse

In our style-conscious society of designer labels gracing every article that a woman wears or carries on her person, we must address the appropriate styles and situations in which it is necessary for a woman to carry a purse or briefcase. The usefulness, size, and function of these important carry-alls have run the gamut over the years of increasing change in women's roles in the workplace and lifestyle traverses. Some feel that they can't go anywhere without one. And some take everything but the kitchen sink in them, creating a possible need for chiropractic adjustments later in life when their shoulder gives out. Then there are the free-spirited women who consider any size purse a great deal of hassle and find them an encumbrance. All in all, there are some rules of thumb that one might consider when looking at the best size for the occasion.

A lady does not carry a bag that could be considered a "lethal weapon" on an airplane or other closely crowded environment as she walks past others. Maneuvering down an aisle with a huge bulky purse that weighs ten or fifteen pounds can slow down the journey and also might injure a seated individual by hitting him or her in the head as she passes by.

Make sure the purse fits the occasion. A small beaded bag is wonderful for weddings or formal events at which a lady is wearing elegant attire.

A moderately sized leather bag is a complementary look for a business cocktail event or lunch meeting. A bulky purse will only be hard to maneuver in a crowd or in a restaurant. (Note: A lady does not place her purse where a waiter might trip over it while serving others at her table.) When calling on a business client, it can be awkward to have both a briefcase *and* a purse to carry to the appointment. Soft-sided briefcases have now been conveniently designed with many compartments and pockets that can serve the purpose of concealing lipstick, credit cards and other small necessities that a woman might need during her business visit.

While traveling on vacation, large purses can be appropriate for making sure that a lady has all her essentials. Transferring a few things to a smaller bag upon entering restaurants or other places for a short time might be the best alternative to carrying such a heavy load on her shoulder during her travels. Some of us call them "date" purses. A little more dainty for the moment, but allowing that she has all her personal needs in a larger purse kept in the car or back at the hotel.

A purse can reflect a lady's personality and attitude for the occasion. It can be as important as the right jewelry some fashion stylists assert. Carrying one in good taste that befits the dress and the social setting gives a lady that special confidence that she enjoys when she knows she looks her best.

A lady knows that her posture is as important as any article of clothing on her back.

❧

A lady does not dump the contents of her purse on the table for all to see.

❧

A lady does not buy clothes a size too small in hopes she will one day be able to wear them.

❧

A lady does not wear strappy sandals and airy open-toed shoes when working in a conservative business environment.

❧

A lady is careful about the jewelry she wears. She should prefer to have someone looking her in the eye instead of watching her earrings swing back and forth during an animated conversation.

❧

A lady gets a pedicure in preparation for the warm weather months.

A lady is mindful of her appearance at all times.

~

If a lady chooses to wear nail polish, she makes sure it is not chipped.

~

A lady never paints her nails in public.

~

A lady doesn't wear white shoes before Easter nor after Labor Day.

~

A lady who colors her hair knows when her roots are showing and makes an appointment with her stylist.

~

If a lady expects her legs to be seen, she either shaves her legs or wears hose.

A Lady Goes on a Date

Over the course of her lifetime, a lady will be presented with many opportunities for dating. And whether her date takes her to an elegant restaurant or a rock concert, a lady knows how to handle herself in every social situation.

Because a lady knows herself, she knows how long it will take her to get ready. And for that reason, a lady is always ready when her date arrives. She knows that reservations, theater curtains, and a lot of men will not wait because she can't decide what to wear. If knowing how to dress for an evening is the problem, the lady asks her date beforehand. Should it be a "first date," a lady should feel free to ask what kind of restaurant they are going to, not only so that she will know how to dress, but also because it gives her the opportunity to let her date know if the restaurant isn't her cup of tea or about any food allergies she may have.

At a restaurant a lady should by all means order what she likes to eat. A lady does not order a small dinner salad when she really wants the pasta. But at the same time, a lady does not order the most expensive item on the menu.

It's a fact of life that not everyone has that special chemistry. Occasionally a lady finds her date is someone with whom she has nothing in common. Only in the case of a potential health risk does a lady complain about the restaurant. But if is it only a matter of boredom, a lady finishes the evening and thanks him. Under no circumstances does a lady feign a headache or suddenly remember a previous engagement.

Throughout the evening (for example when a gentleman pulls her chair out for her or as they are leaving the restaurant), a lady thanks her date. At the end of the evening, a lady thanks her date for inviting her to spend an evening with him.

A lady realizes that the purse she carries (if she carries one at all) makes a statement about her.

~

A lady never adjusts her bra or bustline within view of other people. She also does not let her bra straps show unless they were meant to show.

~

A lady tips the person who shampoos and cuts her hair at her salon, unless it is the owner of the salon.

~

A lady realizes that a hair stylist is not a miracle worker, and by simply showing the stylist a photograph from a magazine, she will not be magically transformed into a supermodel.

A lady knows that her hair makes a statement about her that is equally as important as the clothes she puts on her back.

~

A lady does not use her stylist as a personal counselor. She does not spend her time in the chair recounting her woes in life.

A Lady and Her Luggage

Whether on an overnight business trip or a grand tour of Europe, a lady will find many occasions when she will need to pack a suitcase. Keeping in mind that there may be times when she must handle her own luggage, a lady does not pack her entire wardrobe for a weekend at a country inn. She thinks ahead and takes just enough, with maybe one extra outfit, to get her through her trip.

A lady does not attempt to carry more luggage on an airplane than is allowed by the airline. A lady is also cognizant of the airline's restrictions on weight for checked baggage. If a lady packs 60 pounds of clothing in one suitcase, she pays the extra amount required with a smile on her face. If she is unsure of the number of pieces of luggage allowed, she calls and asks or visits the airline's website to confirm. If a lady is attempting to carry on a piece of luggage that may weigh more than she can comfortably lift herself, she checks it. Although oftentimes there will be a gentleman who will be happy to help a lady with her luggage, she cannot count on this.

Hotels today usually provide hair dryers, irons, and other items that a lady may think of as necessities. Before packing and lugging them around the globe, a lady calls and finds out if the hotel offers these items.

And because mistakes do happen, a lady makes sure her bags are identifiable from others and that her luggage tags are up-to-date in the event of lost luggage.

A lady donates the clothing she no longer wears to those less fortunate than she.

～

A lady owns an evening bag or a small purse for special nighttime events.

～

A lady never asks another lady what her outfit cost or what size it is.

～

A lady does not feel the urge to wear eight rings on one hand.

～

A lady never asks another person if her jewelry is "real."

～

When a lady tries on jeans that do not flatter her, she keeps on shopping until she finds the perfect cut and style for her body type.

～

A lady follows the lead of her supervisor when determining how to dress.

A Lady Gets Dressed

When a lady shops online, she learns their return policies upfront.

⌒

A lady realizes that one designer's size 2 may equate to another designer's size 6. She is especially mindful of that when she is shopping online. Many websites offer sizing charts that can be helpful in figuring this out.

⌒

A lady knows that her travel agent is a fount of knowledge when needing advice on how to dress for a vacation.

⌒

A lady knows whether she has the figure to wear tight clothing. She knows that just because an item of clothing comes in her size does not mean she should wear it.

A Lady Goes to a Wedding

Obviously, a lady only attends weddings to which she has been invited. If her invitation does not say "and guest," she attends alone, even if a reception follows. She arrives on time and sits on the appropriate side of the aisle (the left side if she is a friend of the bride, the right side if she is a friend of the groom; if she knows them both, she sits on the side with the greater number of empty seats). During the ceremony she stands when everyone else does, and she does not chat during the music. At the reception she speaks to the bride and groom and to their parents (no matter how many divorces are involved).

When choosing her attire for a wedding, a lady is careful not to choose anything that will upstage the bride.

〜

A lady realizes that the bride is the star of the show and all attention should be on her.

〜

A lady never wears white to a wedding unless it is her own. She is also mindful that the fabric she is wearing is appropriate for the season. For daytime weddings, a lady chooses a dress or a suit that is softer than her usual business attire. For an early evening wedding, a lady may choose a cocktail dress or a dressier suit. Floor length or three-quarter length dresses are appropriate for formal weddings.

〜

A lady wears clean, fresh underwear.

〜

A lady knows when she needs to wear a slip or a half-slip and does so.

A lady never purchases an item of clothing with the express intent of wearing it once and returning it later.

～

A lady wears hosiery to formal weddings and dinners, as well as in formal business settings.

～

A lady should never ask someone if her clothes maker her look fat.

～

A lady knows that whenever there is a doubt about the color, black is best.

～

A lady knows that trends come and go, while true style is timeless.

～

A lady knows that false congeniality is as obvious as bad false eyelashes.

Even if she doesn't agree with them, a lady does not belittle anyone about wearing fur and leather. If this is an important cause in her life, she volunteers her time and her money to make changes. She does not confront or embarrass others.

Chapter Three

A LADY GOES TO DINNER

Unless absolutely necessary, a lady turns off her cell phone when she goes to dinner. If for some reason, she must leave her phone on because she is expecting a very important call, she lets her fellow diners know in advance. A lady does not take a call while sharing a meal with others unless it is extremely important.

A lady knows when it is acceptable to eat the garnish.

When a lady has an unpleasant time in a restaurant, she does not badger the wait staff. She lodges her complaint with the management. Unless she is a glutton for punishment, she does not go back to that restaurant.

A Lady Leaves a Tip

When a lady is dining alone or with friends and has accepted responsibility for settling the check, she also knows it is her responsibility to leave a tip for the server. A tip of 15 percent of the total bill is expected for good service. A tip of 20 percent or more is justified for superior service. Likewise, if a lady feels the service she or her party has received is inferior, she is justified in leaving 10 percent. At no time does a lady attempt to be cute by leaving a penny or a quarter as a sign of her dissatisfaction.

A lady does not discuss the amount she is tipping with her guests. That decision is between her and the server. But in addition to the monetary tip she leaves, a lady also publicly thanks her server for making her dining experience enjoyable.

Occasionally a lady finds herself in the company of someone who is paying for a meal and leaves an inadequate tip. A lady does not say anything to make her companion feel cheap, but if it continues to be a problem, she may think twice about going to dinner again with that person.

A lady offers to split the dinner tab with a gentleman if she chooses. If he refuses, she graciously accepts his kindness and says, "Thank you."

～

A lady knows when it is acceptable to drink through a straw.

～

A lady sits up straight, especially at the table.

～

A lady does not slurp her soup.

～

A lady shows up on time for her reservation at a restaurant.

～

A lady who does not show up on time for her reservation realizes that not only is she being rude to the other people in her party, she is also putting the entire party at risk of losing their reservation in an especially busy restaurant.

A Lady Goes to Dinner

A lady does not apply makeup at the table. Even in a loud and busy restaurant, a lady does not speak at such a high volume that she attracts attention to her table. She also avoids high-pitched, overloud laughter.

~

A lady does not put her elbows on the table while she is eating.

~

A lady knows that she does not butter an entire piece of bread. She breaks off a piece and butters each as she eats it. The exception to that rule is a hot biscuit or piece of cornbread.

~

When a lady leaves the table, she asks to be excused. She does not need to give her reason for leaving the table.

~

If a lady must cough, burp, or belch, she covers her mouth with her napkin.

~

A lady does not blow her nose at the table.

A lady does not talk about her weight
or how much weight she is going to
gain by eating something she has
ordered at the table.

～

A lady chews her food quietly.

～

When dining in a restaurant, a lady feels
free to ask for a doggy bag or a to-go box.

～

A lady does not ask to taste another
person's food.

～

Should a lady's fellow diner offer a bite of
something on their plate, she feels free to
accept if in doing so she will not make a
mess of the table.

～

When a lady has a bit of food lodged
in her teeth and she cannot remove it
discreetly, she excuses herself from the
table to take care of the situation.

A lady remembers the first name of her server. She realizes that during the course of the evening, any number of employees of the restaurant may assist her, but should she have a question, concern, or complaint, she goes to her server.

⌒

If a lady's meal is slow to arrive from the kitchen, and if others at the table have been served, she urges them, "Please go ahead without me." And she means it.

⌒

If a lady is on a diet, she does not talk about it at the table.

⌒

If a lady has invited a gentleman or any other friend out for dinner, it is her responsibility to make the reservation.

⌒

If a lady has not made a dinner reservation, she accepts the fact that she may have to wait in the bar.

How to Know Which
Fork to Use

If the table has been set correctly, a lady has no problem knowing which fork, spoon, or knife to pick up first. When she sits down at the table, she will find her flatware and her cutlery set out in the order in which she will need it. When the first course arrives, she uses the fork that is farthest away from her plate. When she is finished with that course, she leaves her fork on her plate, and it is taken away. She proceeds in the same manner throughout the meal so that by the time dessert arrives, she will have only one fork, spoon, or knife left. If, by chance, the flatware has been arranged in the wrong order, a lady still follows this logical system. In such cases, the person setting the table has caused the confusion.

A lady does not talk with her mouth full.

❧

A lady knows to start with the fork on the outside. If the salad fork is in the wrong place, she does not make a scene.

❧

When a lady finishes eating, she places her knife and fork on her plate. She never places a piece of dirty flatware back on the table.

❧

Once a lady's dinner utensils have been dirtied, she never lets them touch the tablecloth.

❧

A lady does not salt her food before tasting it. She would never insult the cook in that way.

How to Order a
Bottle of Wine

Occasionally a lady will find herself hosting a dinner at which it will be her responsibility to select a bottle of wine. If she is confident doing this, a lady selects a wine she likes in her price range. If she is not confident doing this, she may feel free to ask her dinner guests or the server for suggestions.

In general, red wine is still the wine of choice to accompany red meat, pasta dishes with tomato sauces, and most heavy entrées. White wines are usually selected to accompany fish, chicken, salads, and pasta dishes with light sauces. However, the hostess may feel free to order any wine she likes.

As hostess, she will be presented the wine by the server, who will show her the label. The server will then offer her the cork, so she can see that it is not too dry. Next, the server will pour a sip of wine in the lady's glass. A lady performs a quick taste test, and if the wine is to her liking, she allows the server to fill the glasses at her table.

The server will leave the white wine in a cooler at tableside and the red wine on the table. In either case, the hostess may wait for the server to return to refill empty glasses, or she may take care of that duty herself.

When a lady pours from a bottle of wine, she finishes by turning the bottle slightly upward, thus preventing drips that might stain.

How to Make a Dinner Reservation

A lady realizes that a dinner reservation is a verbal or online contract between her and the restaurant. She does not make a reservation unless she actually plans to use it, and if she must cancel or if the size of her party changes, she informs the restaurant as far ahead of time as possible.

A lady does not take it personally if a restaurant is unable to seat her party at the time she requests. If she is unable to accept a reservation at an earlier or later hour, a lady asks for a recommendation of another establishment.

If her party has special requirements—a guest who has a physical challenge or a diner with dietary restrictions—a lady makes them known when she reserves the table.

If a hostess, a manager, or a maître d' has been particularly helpful in arranging a lady's reservation, she gladly acknowledges that service with a tip. However, she presents that tip as unostentatiously as possible, perhaps slipping it into the hostess's palm in the midst of a parting handshake.

If a lady does not know the established dress code of a restaurant at which she is planning to dine, she calls ahead. If she is the one extending an invitation to others, she lets them know as well.

⁓

When a lady chooses not to drink wine, she feels perfectly confident in telling the waiter, "No, thank you. I'll just have some water (or some iced tea or soda)."

⁓

At a cocktail party or at a seated dinner, if a lady discovers that she has put something unpleasant, or unpalatable, in her mouth, she gets rid of it in the most efficient way possible. In most cases, she simply uses her fingers or her fork. She works quickly and does not even attempt to disguise her actions behind a napkin.

When faced with a plate of long pasta—such as spaghetti, linguine, or fettuccine—a lady resists every temptation to chop it up with her knife and fork. Instead, she twirls a manageable mouthful around the tines of her fork and, with the help of a spoon, transfers it to her mouth.

~

A lady does not engage in a debate over politics or religion or other sensitive issues at the dinner table.

How to Use a Dinner Napkin

After a lady has been seated, her first action is always to place her dinner napkin in her lap. She does not wait for the server to do so, although in some extremely fancy restaurants, that is done.

If a lady briefly leaves the table during dinner, she leaves the napkin, loosely folded, in the chair. A lady never places her napkin back on the table until she is finished with her meal and about to leave.

A lady tips graciously and as
generously as the service merits.

～

A lady always tips the valet
parking attendant.

～

A lady never assumes that somebody
else will pick up the tab.

～

A lady never dickers over the bill.

～

If separate checks are offered in a
restaurant where a lady is dining with
friends, she asks for them.

～

A lady does not crunch her ice.

～

Although it is customary for a server
to take a lady's order first, if she isn't
prepared, she asks that others in her
party go first, even if she is the only
woman at the table.

A Lady Goes to Dinner

Chapter Four

A LADY SAYS THE RIGHT THING

A lady does not voice strong opinions about controversial topics with total strangers or business associates who she does not know well. A lady knows that people take their opinions and issues very personally at times.

~

A lady consults the dictionary for correct spelling and definitions of words she uses in her conversations and correspondence.

~

A lady does not correct another person's grammar.

~

A lady never curses in front of others.

A lady knows that "please" and "thank you" are still the magic words.

A lady does not brag.

A lady does not whine.

A lady does not nag.

A lady knows how to give a compliment.

A lady knows how to accept a compliment by saying, "Thank you." She never says, "This old thing?" when another person compliments what she is wearing. A lady knows that questioning someone's compliment is akin to questioning their taste.

A lady never insults another person on purpose.

How to Start a Conversation

Whether at a party, a business meeting, or formal occasion, a lady is comfortable striking up a conversation with any pleasant person she chooses. To prevent awkwardness, however, she begins with positive, noncontroversial subject matter. She says, "Isn't this a beautiful home?" or "Isn't the food just wonderful?" If the person responds cordially, she continues with a few more questions until the conversation is under way. A lady knows that she is still testing the waters. In talking with a new acquaintance she does not venture into controversial topics or voice strong politically driven opinions that may lead to an embarrassing moment.

When a lady initiates a telephone
conversation, she knows it is her
responsibility to end that conversation.

A lady never tells jokes that may
embarrass other people, even if those
other people are not in the room.

A lady does not laugh at racist, sexist,
or homophobic jokes.

A lady knows that gossip can harm others
and avoids it at all costs.

A lady always thinks before she speaks.

A lady knows how to make and
accept an apology.

How to End a Conversation

A lady realizes that every conversation must come to an end. And she is not being rude or inconsiderate when she attempts to bring a chat—regardless of how charming her friend is—to a timely close.

When a lady makes a telephone call, she accepts the responsibility for ending that conversation. When a conversation begins in her office or at her work station, it is her obligation to bring that conversation to an end. When on the phone, a lady may simply say, "Elizabeth, I have enjoyed our conversation; I hope we get to talk again soon." In person, she stands up, thanks her guest for meeting with her, and extends her hand for a handshake.

Even in social situations, such as a cocktail party, a lady may end a conversation gracefully by saying, "I have enjoyed getting to know you, Colby. Would you care to walk over to the bar along with me?" This allows the lady an opportunity to introduce Colby to other people. If Colby chooses not to accompany her to the bar, a lady says, "I am so glad we had a chance to talk."

If an apology is sincerely offered, a lady accepts it with good grace. She does not pretend that the offense never existed, but she considers it history and moves on.

A lady does not raise her voice when angry. It is only proper to shout at someone when he or she is in danger or about to score a touchdown.

How to Say, "I'm Sorry"

Although a lady always tries to be considerate of others, she is also human and occasionally makes mistakes. When that happens, a lady recognizes her shortcomings and immediately sets out to correct her wrongdoings.

While an e-mail may seem like the easiest way to apologize, a lady knows that an apology made face to face is best (unless, of course, the apology is being made on the telephone) and is direct and to the point. For example, if she has had a mishap such as spilling a glass of wine on someone's rug, she may say, "Betty, I am so sorry for spilling the wine on your beautiful rug. I feel like such a klutz."

When a lady makes an apology, she means it. She says she is sorry and realizes that the apology does not downplay her mistake. Yet, she need not bring it up again and again. At the same time, a lady never offers an insincere apology, especially if she has done nothing wrong.

A lady uses the phrase "excuse me" as she is moving through a crowded room. She only says "I'm sorry" when an apology is in order.

$\smile$

A lady excuses herself when she is in a public place and needs to make a call on her cell phone.

$\smile$

A lady always returns voice mail as promptly as she possibly can.

$\smile$

A lady never mentions her monthly period or the fact that she has cramps, except to the closest of friends.

How to Make a Complaint

There are times when a lady is perfectly justified in lodging a complaint. If she has received poor service, if she has been treated rudely, or if she has been the target of an undeserved affront, she has every right to make her displeasure known—not only for the sake of her bruised feelings, but also in hopes that the unpleasantness will not occur again.

A lady knows, however, that it is useless to make a complaint unless it is made to the right person. For instance, if a lady has received inferior service in a restaurant, she does not waste her breath complaining directly to the server, who may feel no compulsion to change his behavior. Instead, a lady expresses her concern to the manager or owner of the establishment. If she has the opportunity, she makes her complaint in person; otherwise, she makes a telephone call or puts her concerns in writing.

When a lady makes a complaint, she gives specific reasons for her displeasure. She does not make threats. If she is served poorly at a restaurant or at any other establishment, she may choose not to take her business there again. However, if the poor service continues after she has made her complaint, she does not continue to subject herself to further unpleasantness. She takes her business elsewhere.

A lady never whispers in the presence of others. If she has something to say that cannot be said in the presence of others, she waits until she and the other person are alone.

How to Write a
Sympathy Note

It is appropriate, and even expected, for a lady to express her sympathy upon the death of someone she has known, admired, or respected. She may also wish to express her sympathy to a close friend who has lost a loved one. A lady does this in a simple yet thoughtful way. She may say, "I considered Sophie to be a close friend. I will miss her very much." To comfort a friend's loss, she may write, "I was so sorry to hear of your grandmother's passing. You are in my thoughts."

A lady never says, "Please let me know if there is anything I can do," leaving it up to the grieving person to ask for help. Instead she offers to supply a meal for the family or to pick up the mail while the person is away.

While it is acceptable for a lady to send an "I'm sorry for your loss" message on Facebook or via e-mail, she still attempts to communicate directly with the bereaved friend, either through a handwritten note or in person.

A lady knows that certain questions are too nosy to be asked, such as:

* You don't remember me, do you?
* Where do I know you from?
* Are you and Bob ever going to get married?
* When are you and Bob going to have children?
* How old is Bob?
* How much did those shoes, that dress, that ring, that scarf cost?

When to Use First Names

Although the world at large is on a first-name basis today, a lady knows it is always safe, on first meeting, to address a new acquaintance as "Mr." or "Ms."—especially if she is making her first encounter with that person via telephone or e-mail. She pays particular heed to this guideline if the new acquaintance is an older person or if she is dealing with her superior in a business environment. However, once "Ms. Walters" has told her, "Please, call me Barbara," a lady concedes to her wish. Otherwise, she runs the risk of making her feel ill at ease.

In general, if a lady finds that a person of her own generation is referring to her as "Ms. Ross," she may logically assume that that person wishes to be referred to as "Mr." or "Ms." too. She does not attempt to force business acquaintances to act as if they were her personal friends.

No matter a lady's age or background, she attempts to use proper grammar and pronunciation. If a lady wants to say anything that will be remembered, she knows it is important to say it right.

A lady never claims to have seen a movie she hasn't seen or to have read a book about which she has only read reviews. She knows how to say, "I haven't read (or seen) that yet, but from what I hear about it, it sounds very interesting. What do you think?"

How to Write a
Thank-You Note

A lady knows that it is never wrong to write a thank-you note for any kindness that she has received—whether it is a holiday gift, a night at the symphony, a dinner party in a friend's home, a weekend stay in a friend's cabin, or a ride to the garage to pick up her car. In every case, however, she keeps her thank-you brief and to the point. She specifically mentions the kindness she has received. ("The book was a perfect gift. The author is one of my favorites." "The concert was wonderful. I love Yo-Yo Ma." "I don't know how I'd ever have made it to work if you hadn't given me a lift to the Auto Outlet.")

Chapter Five

A LADY GIVES A PARTY

A lady may use her best china or dinnerware to serve her guests if she chooses. If something breaks, she is not disturbed and does not allow her guests to feel any guilt over the matter.

⌣

If a guest offers to bring the wine or to help in some other way with the dinner menu, a lady may either accept or decline the offer. Either way, she says, "Thank you," and means it.

⌣

A lady does not extend last-minute invitations to a party she has been planning for some time.

A lady is careful about answering her telephone during a party she is hosting. It may be necessary for her to answer the phone in the event one of her guests is lost or will not be able to attend. Should the call be for any other reason, a lady always asks if she can return the call later and returns her attention to her guests.

~

A lady does not need to write a thank-you note for a gift that was given to her at her own party. She knows that the gift was meant as a thank-you for hosting the party.

~

If a lady wants her guests to leave, she puts away the liquor.

~

If a guest arrives with a bottle of wine, a lady is not obligated to serve it. She accepts it as a gift to be enjoyed at her discretion.

How to Set Up a Bar

A lady does not stock her bar in order to impress people. She stocks her bar with the libations people actually want to drink. For even the largest, most eclectic group, a choice of Scotch, vodka, gin, white wine, and, in the South, bourbon will suffice. What is more, her guests will find themselves much less confused.

In every case, a lady makes sure to have ample ice, and she offers a variety of mixers, not just for the pleasure of her drinking friends, but out of consideration for her teetotaling guests as well. Quality, a lady knows, is always more important than quirkiness.

A lady knows that her bar is never complete without sliced limes and lemons, a jigger, a stirrer, and a tall stack of hand-ironed, starched cotton cocktail napkins.

Help Wanted

If a lady feels she will need assistance in throwing a party, particularly if it is a large gathering, or if she is less than confident in her skills behind the bar or in the kitchen, she engages the services of a bartender, a caterer, or both.

Before hiring help for a party, a lady seeks the advice of friends whose hosting skills she respects. If she is inexperienced when it comes to throwing parties, she is not ashamed to ask how much she should expect to pay for top-flight service. She knows it is wise to contact the bartender or caterer well ahead of time, since the best people in those professions are often fully booked, especially during the holidays. She also knows that she may need to make more than one call in order to find servers who fit her budget.

In her consultations with a potential caterer or bartender, a lady makes it clear how many people she is inviting to her party, offers an idea as to the menu she would like to serve, and is careful to outline the service she expects. For instance, she makes it clear whether she wants the servers to pass drinks or hors d'oeuvres, or whether she merely expects them to serve from behind the bar or set out the buffet. She lets them know what time she expects them to arrive and how long the party will last. She makes sure they understand whether she expects them to bring the ice or whether she will be providing it herself.

In her first conversation with a caterer or a bartender, a lady asks, straightforwardly, how much she will be charged and if their services are available for the date of her event. If the estimate is beyond her budget, or if she is not happy with the menu suggestions she is offered, she says, "Thank you so much, but this isn't quite what I had in mind. Maybe we can work together another time."

Once she has engaged the services of a caterer, she depends on the caterer for advice. She will quickly learn that an experienced, well-connected caterer can be invaluable. She will also find that caterers can provide their own serving dishes and will even engage and supervise the bartenders. In every circumstance, a lady can expect the caterers to stay until the established closing time for the party and to leave her home (especially her kitchen) cleaner than it was when they arrived.

If she is paying a set fee to her bartenders or her caterer, she does not tip them. If she wishes to do so, she may tip any servers who have come to assist the caterer, but she does not permit them to set out tip jars at a party in her home.

A lady makes sure to exchange cell phone numbers with the bartenders and the caterer, in case she needs answers to last-minute questions or should emergencies arise.

A lady always serves food when serving alcohol to offset its effects.

A lady makes it a point to know the names of the teams playing in the Super Bowl.

A lady makes a point to ask her dinner guests if they have any dietary restrictions she should consider before planning her menu.

A lady does not give surprise birthday parties or baby or bridal showers unless she is certain the honoree likes to be surprised.

A lady makes sugar-free sweeteners and low-calorie creamers available to her guests.

How to Seat a Table

If a lady entertains—whether in her home or in a public place—the moment will come when she will be expected to "seat" a table. At that moment, she, as a hostess, will be asked to decide where each of her guests will sit during the meal. A lady takes this obligation seriously, knowing that her decisions will make or break the evening. She attempts to seat compatible guests beside each another, but she never seats a couple—whether they are married, a long-standing couple, or on a first date—side by side. Her goal is to create a mix of guests who will ask one another questions, generating lively conversation.

If there is a guest of honor, that person is always given the best seat. At a banquet, for example, the honored guest is given the seat with the best view of the room. In a private home, the guest of honor is seated at the hostess's right hand or, better yet, between two particularly congenial guests.

Meanwhile, a hostess reserves for herself the least desirable seat. For instance, at a formal dinner where there are to be speeches, she takes the seat with the poorest view of the podium. Her compensatory reward comes from watching the happy faces of her handsomely entertained guests.

A lady always sets the table before her guests arrive.

A lady is not required to open a hostess gift in the presence of the giver unless she desires to do so.

About Flowers and Candles

A romantic dinner table really needs fresh flowers and the soft glow of candles. But the flowers should be an asset to the table, not an obstruction. A lady arranges them in a low vase or bowl, so they do not hamper eye contact between her and her guest. She shies away from overly aromatic blooms such as heavy-scented lilies, which can overpower even the strongest passion.

Candlelight makes anybody look more attractive, including the lady herself. As with flowers, candles should be positioned so that they are not an obstacle or a safety hazard. The hostess lights them just before serving the salad course, and she makes sure to snuff them out before leaving the table. (When snuffing out candles, she cups one hand behind the flame, to prevent hot wax from spattering across the table and onto her guest.)

In order to make sure that her candles can be easily lighted, a clever hostess tests them ahead of time, letting them burn for a few minutes so that some of the wax slides away from the wick.

If a guest offers to help clean up after the party, a lady may either accept or decline the offer. However, she has no reason to expect that such an offer will be made.

❧

A lady makes sure that her invitation, whether it comes by telephone, by mail, or by e-mail, provides all the necessary information. She gives the time, the date, the location, and the expected attire.

❧

If a lady sends her invitations by e-mail, she should know that some people do not check their e-mail as religiously as others.

How to Set a Dinner Table

A lady knows how to set an elegant, if rudimentary, dinner table. The basic equipment is arranged in this manner:

When salad is served as a first course

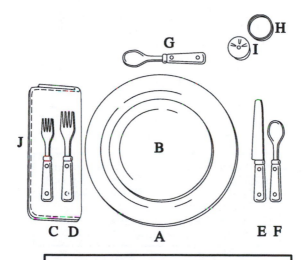

A. Dinner Plate
B. Salad Plate
C. Salad Fork
D. Dinner Fork
E. Dinner Knife
F. Coffee Spoon
G. Dessert Spoon*
H. Water Glass
I. Wine Goblet
J. Napkin

The Dessert Spoon can be a fork, if appropriate.

When salad is served along with the entrée

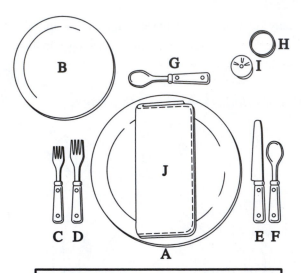

A. Dinner Plate	F. Coffee Spoon
B. Salad Plate	G. Dessert Spoon*
C. Salad Fork	H. Water Glass
D. Dinner Fork	I. Wine Goblet
E. Dinner Knife	J. Napkin

The Dessert Spoon can be a fork, if appropriate.

A lady does not hesitate to invite her guests into the kitchen as she finishes preparations for her dinner.

～

A lady is always ready before her first guest arrives. She does not answer the door in her robe, or half made-up.
If lady is still making last minute adjustments to the food, she encourages her guests to begin the first course.

～

A lady clearly lets her guests know where to park.

～

A lady lets her neighbors know when she is hosting a large number of people, especially if she has a limited amount of parking near her home.

How to Serve Dinner

Before a lady's guests arrive, she has already placed the dinner plates, flatware, and glasses on the table. Once the guests have chatted for a bit and have perhaps had a drink of some sort, she suggests that they proceed to the table. Thereafter, the procedure is as follows:

- The guests take their places.

- If a lady is serving a salad, she places the salad plates directly on the dinner plates (which have already been set).

- When the guests have finished their salads, a lady removes the salad plates. If she plans to serve the dinner plates in the kitchen, she takes them away at the same time. The salad forks should remain on the guests' salad plates.

- A lady either serves the dinner plates in the kitchen, or she brings the main course and its side dishes to the table, where the guests serve themselves.

- When guests have finished the main course, with second helpings if they are offered, a lady takes away the dinner plates along with the dinner forks and knives.

- Finally, a lady serves dessert. If she has not already placed the dessert forks or spoons on the table, she may bring them out along with the dessert itself. If there is coffee, she serves it now.

- If the dinner conversation continues after her guests have finished their desserts, a lady takes the empty plates away and pours more coffee. She never, never rushes her friends to leave the table after a satisfying meal.

A lady realizes that her guests are
her primary concern.

～

If a lady is hosting a party alone, she does
not hesitate to ask a friend to help greet
her guests and show them where to put
their coats and purses.

～

A lady realizes it is her responsibility if her
guests become inebriated. She arranges
for them to be driven home by a sober
friend or a cab. She takes away a guest's
car keys if she has to.

～

When a guest behaves less than mannerly,
a lady endures the actions of her guest,
but she remembers those actions the next
time she makes out her guest list.

Chapter Six

A LADY GOES TO A PARTY

A lady considers any invitation an act of generosity and kindness. She accepts or declines it as promptly and as graciously as possible.

◦—◦

If a lady finds that her schedule will allow her to stop in at more than one event on the same day or evening, she does so. She explains to her host or hostess ahead of time, however, that such will be the case. If she is invited to a dinner party and will not be able to stay for the actual dinner, she is scrupulous in making her intentions clear.

If prior experience has taught a lady to expect unpleasant behavior, or even illegal behavior (such as drinking and driving or drug use), on the part of her host or hostess, or their usual group of friends, she declines their invitation politely, saying, "I wish I could join you, Morris, but I already have an engagement that evening." A lady knows that this is the whitest lie possible. Even if she merely plans to stay home and read a book, that still constitutes an "engagement."

⌣

If a lady is not sure what the dress code for the evening is, she simply asks her host or hostess.

⌣

A lady feels free to use the hand towel in the powder room.

⌣

A lady never asks to turn on the television, change the music, or turn off the music at another person's party.

When a lady is offered a name tag,
she puts it on.

～

A lady never waits for something
better to come along.

～

A lady is never the last to leave a party.
Neither, if she can avoid it, is she the
first to arrive.

～

If a lady is concerned that she will
be the only "uncoupled" person at
a party, she informs the host of the
party ahead of time.

～

A lady does not dispose of her
feminine hygiene products at
another person's home.

～

A lady knows what "RSVP" means
and always responds to invitations
bearing that request.

A LADY GOES TO A PARTY

If a lady discovers she can attend a party for which she has already declined an invitation, she calls her host and asks if she may attend.

⁓

Once a lady discovers that she must decline an invitation that she has already accepted, she promptly lets her host or hostess know. She gives a frank explanation for her change of plans and offers a sincere apology.

How to Respond to an Invitation

A lady wastes no time in responding to an invitation. If she sees the letters RSVP (an abbreviation for the French equivalent of "Please reply"), she is obligated to respond, either by telephone, in writing, or via e-mail if an e-mail address is provided. An RSVP requires that she reply whether or not she plans to attend the event in question. If the directive is "Regrets only," she need only inform her host or hostess if she does not plan to attend.

A lady understands that it is terribly inconsiderate for her not to make her intentions known.

If a lady must decline an invitation, she gives a straightforward reason for doing so. "I have a prior engagement," "I will have guests from out of town," and "I will be away on vacation" are all perfectly acceptable explanations.

A lady does not lay down conditions for her accepting an invitation. She does not ask, "What will you be serving?" or "Who else is going to be there?" She accepts the invitation gladly and proves to herself that, because she is a lady, she can have a good time in any company, at any time.

A lady does not take a date to a party unless she is expected to do so. If her invitation is not addressed to her "and guest," she does not have the license to bring a guest.

❧

Even if a lady is not having wine or a cocktail, she still raises her glass if a toast is being made. She realizes that even a glass of water, raised in the right spirit, expresses a wish for good luck.

❧

If an invitation says, "Regrets only," a lady only lets the host or hostess know that she does not plan to attend.

❧

At a party, a lady never spends all her time talking to one person. She is always excited to meet as many people as possible, and she assumes that a great many people will enjoy meeting her, too.

If a lady does not see an ashtray, she does not smoke—and she does not ask if she may do so.

⁓

A lady uses a coaster, or a cocktail napkin.

⁓

A lady picks up any large food crumbs that she may have dropped—especially if they could cause a stain if another guest were to step on them.

⁓

A lady is friendly to bartenders at a private party, but she is not required to leave tips for them. That is the responsibility of the host.

⁓

If valet parking is being provided at a party, a lady pulls into line and waits her turn. She is sure to leave the keys in the ignition.

If a lady has too much to drink at a party, she does not drive home. She asks another guest or the host of the party to help her find a way home.

~

A lady knows how to introduce a friend to a stranger at a party. Likewise, a lady knows how to tactfully excuse herself from the company of a party guest when she wishes to seek other companionship.

When to Take a Gift

When a lady is invited to someone's home—for dinner, a holiday party, or for an overnight visit—she knows to take a gift. For a dinner party, she may take flowers, or a bottle of wine (unchilled, so that the host or hostess knows that it is a gift and is not intended to accompany dinner). For a holiday party, she may take a bag of coffee beans, or maybe something she has made herself, such as cookies or an ornament. If she is invited for a longer period of time—such as a weekend—a lady takes a more substantial gift, such as a coffee table book or a useful kitchen gadget.

A lady always presents her gift directly to her host or hostess. Even though she takes a gift, a lady still sends a thank-you note at her earliest opportunity.

If a lady feels uncomfortable at a party because of the actions of other guests, she explains to her host that she needs to leave and thanks the host for a wonderful evening.

~

If a lady breaks something at a party, she informs the host or hostess and apologizes. She does not attempt to pay for the item. If she wishes, she replaces the item and presents it at another time.

~

A lady knows when it's time to say good night.

~

Even if a lady has brought flowers or wine to a dinner, she still writes a thank-you note.

When to Send a
Thank-You Note

There are many reasons a lady writes a thank-you note. The acknowledgment of a gift or to express appreciation for a kind word or deed are just a couple of reasons. A lady knows that even though she brought a bottle of wine to a party she still writes a note. (The wine says, Thank you for inviting me. The note says, I had a wonderful time.)

A lady is prompt in writing thank-you notes—within ten days of receiving a gift if at all possible. Writing a note lets the giver know in a tangible way just how grateful she is for his or her generosity. The extra effort to write a thank-you note speaks volumes about a lady's courtesy.

A lady need not reply to a thank-you note.

If a lady does not wish to drink alcohol at a party, she politely refuses drinks offered to her and asks for a non-alcoholic beverage.

⌒

If a lady finds she has overdressed or underdressed for a party, she does not leave in a panic. She rises to the occasion and lets her personality and charm be the most noticeable thing about her. But hopefully she has learned an important lesson and will ask the host the proper attire for an event.

⌒

A lady always blots her lipstick well before going out so that she does not leave heavy lipstick marks on her linen napkin, wine glass, or the cheek of a friend she greets. Lipstick marks are never easy to clean and sometimes make the wrong impression.

In the event a lady attends a party at which someone is wearing a dress identical to hers, she simply smiles and compliments the other lady on her excellent choice in clothing.

⌒

A lady never shows up *with* or *as* an uninvited guest to a party.

Chapter Seven

A LADY AND HER FRIENDS

A lady is observant of the habits and lifestyle of friends she is visiting. She does not stay up late if her host is an early riser.

A lady makes up her bed when she stays overnight at someone's home.

A lady never says or does things that make others feel small.

A lady never assumes that people know each other. She always makes introductions and is ready to give her own name first.

A lady does not lend more money than she can afford to lose or borrow more money than she can pay back.

$\sim$

A lady accepts no for an answer, the first time she hears it.

A lady knows that signs of friendship come in many forms. A warm hug or a quick kiss on the cheek is always nice when meeting or leaving a friend. These gestures are never appropriate at business encounters. A lady knows that a firm and genuine handshake paired with a sincere smile will serve her well and take her far.

A lady does not engage in public displays of affection that might embarrass others.

Unless she is invited to a friend's birthday party, a lady feels comfortable simply sending a card. She does her best to keep a record of her friends' birthdays so her cards can go out on time.

～

Unless she is invited to a party in their honor, a lady does not feel compelled to give anniversary gifts to friends who are not related to her.

～

A lady may learn that a bride and groom, a bar or bat mitzvah, or the honorees at a birthday or anniversary gathering, have asked that donations be sent to a specific charitable organization, in lieu of gifts. If that is the expressed desire of the honorees, a lady respects their wishes.

～

Unless she is giving a gift to a young person, about whose taste and hobbies she has no clue, a lady avoids giving a gift certificate, a phone card, or a purchase card, except as a very last resort.

A Lady Sends Flowers

Flowers and being a lady go hand in hand when it comes time to mark a special occasion. Be it a happy time or a sad one, a lady knows that flowers are almost always the right means of expressing her sentiments to a friend or associate. There are many different occasions on which a lady is correct to send flowers: The birth of a child, a promotion or a new job for an associate or coworker, a hostess gift sent ahead of the party, a death in a friend or associate's family, a friend or family member's stay in the hospital, or even a bouquet to say, "I'm sorry I hurt your feelings." There are many reasons to send beautiful flowers to brighten someone's day and show you care.

Tips for sending flowers and ordering them with finesse:

* If a lady is not familiar with a reliable, yet affordable florist, she asks a knowledgeable friend or coworker whom to call. She then states clearly to the florist the maximum dollar amount she wishes to spend on the delivered bouquet. She also describes the type of occasion, in hopes of receiving helpful suggestions from the seasoned florist.

* A lady knows the appropriate time to send flowers to people of different faiths and religions. For instance, a lady would not send flowers to a Jewish family who is sitting Shiva. A lady always considers the appropriate condolence gesture for each religion or family faith.

* When a lady considers sending flowers as a condolence for a death, she does her research to be sure that the family has not made a request for contributions to a favorite charity in lieu of flowers. If there is a request to send a donation to a charity, the lady

writes a note of condolence, including a simple mention of her contribution.

* A very close family friend or relative may certainly send flowers despite the request to make a donation, although she does not send them to the church or funeral home. A casual acquaintance should honor the "in lieu of" request.

* A lady may always spearhead a group of friends, neighbors, coworkers, or lodge members, who might wish to help the bereaved family with funeral expenses if she has good reason to believe they are financially challenged.

* A lady sends flowers to her hostess, preferably before the party, so that her hostess may display the flowers during the party or gathering. She knows that after-the-fact flowers are a generous gesture as well.

A lady is patient with her friends and tolerant of their individual quirks. She knows that a good friend, no matter how quirky, is worth holding close to her heart for life.

⁓

If a lady finds she must raise a sensitive subject with a friend or coworker, she does so in the kindest, but most direct, manner possible.

⁓

If a lady finds she must discuss a sensitive subject with a friend or coworker, she does so in private.

How to Make an Introduction

Even in our increasingly casual society, a lady respects the time-honored traditions surrounding social introductions:

- A younger person is always introduced to an older person. For example, when Perry George, who is in his twenties, is introduced to Mrs. Caldwell, who is in her fifties, a lady says, "Mrs. Caldwell, I'd like you to meet Perry George." Even if a younger woman is being introduced to an older man, a lady makes sure to say the older person's name first.

- When a lady introduces a man and a woman who are of essentially the same age, she introduces the man to the woman. Thus, if her friends Angie Reese and Perry George do not know each other, a lady introduces them by saying, "Angie, this is my friend, Perry George." Then the lady turns to Perry and says, "Perry, this is Angie Reese."

- In all cases, a lady feels free to add some detail to stimulate conversation. She might, for example, say, "Mrs. Caldwell, Perry is one of my good friends from law school." Or, "Angie, you may have heard me talk about Perry. We went to the Mozart concert last week."

- A lady makes every effort to pronounce names clearly. If it is convenient, she repeats the names at some not-too-distant point in the conversation.

- Even if she is uncertain of the protocol of the moment, however, a lady always does her best to make an introduction. Even if she makes a small mistake, she has not committed the more serious mistake of being rude.

A lady uses the word "partner" when introducing an acquaintance to two friends who live together. She realizes the term denotes a special relationship that is beyond "boyfriend," "girlfriend," or "roommate." A lady takes the lead from listening how the couple refer to each other.

~

A lady knows that when faced with a question as to how to treat another person in any situation, she attempts to treat that person as she would wish to be treated.

~

A lady doesn't bombard her friends with useless e-mails.

~

A lady does not assume her friends are interested in having a lengthy telephone conversation just because she wants to talk.

How to Deal with Nondrinkers

Every lady will have friends who at times cannot, or choose not to, drink alcohol. Whatever the reason—religious belief, health, addiction, medication—a lady respects it and never pressures anyone to drink. At the same time, she does not ask why a person is not drinking—and has plenty of delicious nonalcoholic options available.

If a lady chooses not to drink alcohol, she does not impose her decision on other people. If she is offered a glass of wine, she simply says, "No, thank you, but I would love some ginger ale." She offers no further explanation.

How to Shake Hands

A lady may feel free to shake hands with anyone to whom she is introduced—whether at a party or in a business setting. A lady always extends her hand to a gentleman first, letting him know that she wishes to shake his hand. If she does not, then she should not expect the gentleman to extend his hand either. A gentleman has been trained to wait for a lady to extend her hand first should she wish to shake hands.

A lady offers a firm clasp. She does not offer a full-fledged up-and-down pump but a quick, gentle press. She makes sure her hands are dry and clean and looks the person in the eye as she greets him or her or says her goodbyes.

When a lady realizes that another lady's bra strap is showing or she has a piece of toilet paper stuck to her high heel, she discreetly tells her about it as soon as possible.

⌣

A lady is always on time. She knows how long it takes her to get ready and does not keep others waiting. If she is going to be late, she phones ahead and asks the host or hostess to begin the meal without her.

⌣

A lady breaks a date only for reasons of sickness, death, or natural disaster. If she must cancel her plans, she does so with as much advance notice as possible.

⌣

A lady allows others to finish their thoughts and sentences.

⌣

A lady does not hesitate to dispel false rumors about her friends.

A lady lets the gentlemen friends in her life know she appreciates their behavior toward her.

❧

A lady is considerate of the special needs of senior citizens and physically challenged people. For example, if she encounters a blind person who seems confused by a busy street corner, she asks, "May I help you across the street?" If the offer is accepted, the lady provides a helpful hand. If the offer is declined, she maintains her distance, keeping a watchful eye.

❧

A lady opens the door for others entering a building behind her, even for men.

❧

A lady does not give up her friends when she falls in love. Nor does she lose sight of who she is apart from the relationship.

A lady knows how to break up from relationships, leave jobs, and confront friends without losing friendships.

~

A lady knows that the ability to provide an ear to listen or a shoulder to cry on is one of the greatest gifts she can give a friend.

~

A lady is careful when loaning money to others, even close friends. If she does not feel comfortable making the loan, she does not. If she feels a legal agreement will ease her comfort level, she consults an attorney.

How to Be a Houseguest

As a guest in a private home a lady treats her host's furniture and other belongings with the greatest care, even more carefully than if they were her own.

If there are servants who provide some special service for her, or if she stays any great length of time, she shows her gratitude by leaving a thank-you tip.

In every case, a lady attempts to fit into the household routine. She rises and retires according to the household schedule. She eats what is served and does not complain. She makes her bed in the morning, and she disposes of damp towels as instructed.

Above all else, she sticks to her arrival and departure plans. When her visit is over, she checks her room to make sure she has packed all her belongings. She leaves nothing but pleasant memories behind.

A lady does not make phone calls to anyone during the dinner hour.

A lady is not afraid to carry breath mints. Neither is she reluctant to offer them to other people.

A lady never asks anyone to divulge his or her age.

A lady knows that the choice to reveal her own age is entirely up to her.

A lady celebrates her friends and lets them know their importance in her life.

A lady never begins a statement with "I don't mean to embarrass you, but . . ."

How to Deal with Unmarried Couples

A lady may have many friends and acquaintances who live together in nontraditional relationships. If a lady decides to make these people a part of her life, she accepts them as they are, recognizing that their private lives are their business and no one else's. If she does not approve of their behavior, she does not preach to them. Instead, she associates with them as seldom as possible.

In no case does she mention their relationship when introducing them to other people. For example, a lady does not say, "This is Mary Brown, and this is her live-in boyfriend [or "her significant other" or "the father of her child"], Sam Jones." Instead, she says, "I'd like you to meet my friends Mary Brown and Sam Jones."

If the couple feels the need to provide any further details about their living arrangement, they may do so, although in most cases they will be telling people more than they really need or want to know.

In written correspondence with Mary and Sam, a lady addresses the envelope to "Ms. Mary Brown and Mr. Sam Jones." A letter to Bob and Keith would be addressed to "Mr. Bob Grainger and Mr. Keith Harris." Kate and Helen's letter would go to "Ms. Helen Thompson and Ms. Kate Williams," listing them in alphabetical order.

A lady never asks her friends in need what she can do for them. It is better for a lady to respond to a need she sees than expect her friend to come up with a job for her.

～

A lady knows how to be a friend to other ladies as well as to gentlemen.

～

A lady knows when saying "Thank you" is enough and when a bouquet of flowers is appropriate.

～

A lady knows that it is possible to offer assistance to a gentleman without threatening his masculinity.

～

A lady is never overly effusive when complimenting one friend in the presence of others.

How to Deal with Divorced Friends

A lady regrets seeing any loving relationship break up, especially if she considers both persons to be her friends. However, her regret is for their pain, not for her own discomfort. She does not take sides in their marital strife; she does not carry tales back and forth between the opposing camps.

If her friends are recently divorced, a lady does not attempt to put them in situations—a small dinner party, for example—where they will be forced to encounter each other. She tries to maintain communication with both parties, but she understands that she is now friends with two people, not with a couple. Maintaining these friendships may require twice as much effort—and twice as much time.

After a reasonable amount of time has passed, however, a lady may feel free to include both friends in the same event, especially when a good many other people are involved. To forestall any anxiety, though, she is thoughtful enough to make sure both parties are informed ahead of time. She also makes sure that her guest list includes other single people, so that the divorced person does not feel like a fifth wheel.

A lady may say to Betsy, formerly married to Tom, "It's going to be fun, Betsy. I've invited Jim and Marcia, and Bob, Jim, Gloria, Ted and Vivian. I'm going to ask Tom too."

Because a lady's friends are well-mannered people, they would never ask her for such information ahead of time. However, a lady understands if, given the circumstances, they choose to decline her invitation. Only in such extraordinary circumstances, after all, would a well-mannered person ever decline.

Chapter Eight

A LADY GOES TO THE OFFICE

A lady never assumes she can address
her boss by her or his first name until
she has been directed to do so.

⌒

If a lady is in the position to supervise
the work of other people in her office,
she does not attempt to dictate. Instead,
she directs with confidence, wisdom, and
respect for the people she is leading.

⌒

A lady always shows respect, not only
for her superiors, but also for those
who work for her.

A lady does not gossip.

⌇

A lady knows how to make a complaint about her job. She does so by going to her immediate supervisor.

⌇

A lady knows how to dress appropriately for the workplace. If she is to be taken seriously and respected, she must project that sense of style and posture. It starts from within and should be reflected on the outside as well. A lady should not send conflicting messages to clients and coworkers.

⌇

A lady avoids sexist and racist terminology.

⌇

When a lady is asked to take a message or accept a package for a fellow employee, she does so. She makes certain that she takes the message accurately, and she treats the package with care.

A lady always makes sure any delivery she accepts gets into the proper hands, perhaps sending an e-mail to the fellow employee saying, "Dear Jerry, I have a package for you in my office."

⌒

A lady realizes that the office refrigerator is not the place to conduct scientific experiments. She remembers to dispose of her leftovers before they begin to smell.

⌒

On a job interview, a lady dresses as she would for a day at the office. In that way she makes it clear that she understands the nature of the business.

⌒

A lady does not try to get around her company's dress code. She follows the dress code without complaining.

⌒

A lady is not late for meetings.

A lady never asks a coworker, especially not one of her employees, to make the coffee. If she is a coffee drinker, she learns how to operate the coffeemaker herself.

If a lady drinks the last cup of coffee, she makes a new pot.

If a lady is the last to leave the office at the end of the day, she turns the coffeepot off.

When leaving on a business trip with other colleagues, a lady shows up on time.

If a lady is asked whether she wishes to share a hotel room while on a business trip, she makes her preference known. If company policy requires sharing rooms, she behaves courteously and considerately to her roommate.

The Etiquette of Voice Mail

A lady never assumes that anyone recognizes her voice on her messages. She speaks clearly, identifies herself, and leaves her phone number. Better yet, she speaks slowly and gives her number twice. In no case does a lady go on and on. She leaves her message and then gets on with her life. If she needs to have a conversation, she can have one in person.

When a lady's phone message is not returned in a timely fashion and a deadline is involved, she calls back and, if necessary, leaves a second message. It is then the other person's responsibility to return the call.

If a lady receives a message that involves a deadline, such as a meeting time, she returns the message promptly.

When leaving a voice message, a lady conveys a smile through her voice and a cheerful tone when speaking over the phone. She does not leave a message that is tempered with anger or negative emotions.

A lady should keep her workplace conversations to a minimum and always on target with her business at hand.

A lady should never leave someone on hold for more than three minutes in a personal or professional setting. If she cannot secure the information or the person that the caller has requested, then she comes back on the line and takes down the information she will need to pass along. A lady knows that any caller's time is valuable and that leaving them on hold can create a bad impression for the company and also for her own lack of thoughtfulness.

A Lady and Her Boss

A lady realizes that in some situations, there is still a chain of command. While she may be on a first-name basis with her employer and they may go to the same aerobics class, she still remembers who is in charge at the office.

When in a social situation, such as having drinks after work, she accepts without resistance her boss's offer to pick up the tab. If she chooses not to accept an invitation from her boss for an after-work-hours social event, she expresses her gratitude for the invitation nonetheless.

If a lady is entertained in her boss's home, she treats her boss and her boss's spouse just as she would treat any other host or hostess. She takes a small gift if it seems appropriate and always writes a thank-you note—which is sent to their home. (She does not place the note on her boss's desk the next morning.)

If a lady receives a gift from her boss, she accepts it and expresses her gratitude. She understands that her boss does not expect a gift in return. A lady realizes that the gift acknowledges a job well done; it does not suggest an exchange between friends.

If a lady finds that breaks with other workers are only excuses to gossip, she avoids taking breaks with her coworkers.

~

A lady does not talk excessively about business at a social event. She leaves that to regular business hours during the week.

~

A lady offers to help her coworkers who must be off work because of religious or health reasons. These favors go a long way in showing appreciation of others.

~

A lady stands when introduced to others at the office.

~

A lady keeps her address book—whether it is on her computer or in her desk drawer—up to date.

A lady learns the names of receptionists, administrative assistants, and employees at the offices where she makes frequent calls. She thanks them for their assistance as often as possible.

~

A lady makes it a point to ask for an introduction to the wife or girlfriend of a married friend or coworker. Workplace friendships are easy to begin and a lady must be careful to always keep her friendship with a married man in its proper place and context.

~

A lady speaks pleasantly and with a friendly tone when on the telephone. She does not put people on hold for extended periods of time.

~

A lady realizes that the more professionally she presents herself in the workplace, the more seriously she will be taken.

A lady does not smack her
gum at the office.

⌒

A lady is careful how she acts at the
yearly office party.

⌒

A lady writes a thank-you note after
a job interview.

⌒

If a lady must leave her job, for whatever
reason, she does so graciously, expressing
appreciation to management for her
learning experience with that company.

⌒

A lady shows up on time for work.

A Lady and Her Assistant

A lady treats her secretary or administrative assistant, as well as every member of her staff, with the respect due a valued coworker and a fellow human being. She makes her expectations clearly known, and she readily expresses her gratitude for a job well done.

A lady is careful to keep the line clearly drawn between her personal and professional life. If her level of trust is great enough, she may ask her assistant to make her bank deposits for her in an emergency, but she does not take advantage of her assistant with tasks she simply would rather not do, like picking up her cleaning.

A lady may give her assistant a gift on special occasions—such as Administrative Professional's Day or a birthday—but it is always wise to stick with an impersonal item. A lady does not expect a gift in return.

And regardless of the length of the relationship between boss and assistant, a lady never forgets that "please" and "thank you" are the magic words.

A lady always asks business associates if they are busy before she begins a conversation.

～

A lady does not give out business cards at personal parties or events such as weddings. If someone asks her for her card at such an outing, she fulfills his or her request.

～

When a lady changes her office address, e-mail address, or phone number, she informs her business associates as quickly as possible.

～

A lady shares her home phone number, personal cell phone number, or personal e-mail address only with those business associates who really need it. Except in extraordinary circumstances, she does not divulge the home phone numbers, personal cell numbers, or personal e-mail addresses of people who work with her.

If a lady discovers, during a large business meeting, that she needs to use the restroom, she leaves the room quietly. She does not need to announce where she is going or when she plans to return. When she must leave a small meeting, and it is conspicuous, she excuses herself, saying, "I'll be back in a few minutes."

～

A lady does her part to keep the ladies' room at her office as sanitary as possible.

～

A lady does not write personal correspondence on her business stationery.

～

A lady does not lie on her résumé.

～

A lady always restocks the copy machine with paper.

～

A lady does not abuse the privileges of her expense account.

When a lady entertains a business client, even if the client is also a lady, it is her responsibility to pick up the tab.

～

A lady always keeps business cards in her desk and her briefcase. She keeps them in a case and makes sure they are clean and not bent.

The Etiquette of E-Mail

A lady treats e-mail like any other written correspondence. She expresses herself clearly and concisely. She does not send lengthy sequences of short, inconsequential messages that clutter up the recipient's e-mail directory. She indicates the topic of her correspondence in the "Subject" line of her e-mail, so that the recipient can identify it quickly.

If a lady is sending a copy of her e-mail to a second correspondent, she indicates that she is sending a copy in the same way that she would use "cc:" at the bottom of a letter. She knows e-mail is never completely private since it is read on a computer screen and often in an office environment. To save embarrassment to herself and her correspondent, she is discreet about the messages she sends.

When sending an informal e-mail to a close friend, a lady may be casual in her correspondence, but when sending an e-mail for business purposes, a lady pays close attention to her grammar and tone.

A lady knows that writing in uppercase and lowercase sensitive letters can change the feel of the message. She knows it is always wiser to write in complete sentences and not in informal terms.

A lady knows the importance of changing the subject in each of her e-mail responses. When the topic changes the subject line should change as well, helping to keep the stream of conversations clear. Attention to this sort of detail can prove very helpful when researching past e-mail conversations and the important information included in them.

A lady realizes that everything she writes within an e-mail, and sends, will be public knowledge for the world to see should anyone choose to circulate it. Her tone, her comments, her whole reputation is summed up in her written words. A lady should always read carefully what she has written, giving it serious thought and consideration, before she hits the send button.

Social Network Sites—
Using Them Wisely

In recent years, online and business social networks have increased in popularity at a staggering rate. These networks have expanded a lady's opportunities for sharing personal and professional information, as well as ideas that may open a vast array of new horizons in her life. A lady knows that the rules of etiquette still apply and remembers these rules in her online networking relationships.

When a lady adds a friend to her social or business network, she is sure to respect their privacy, and the privacy of all her network contacts, before posting information about them. Some friends prefer to keep certain information personal and have no desire to share it with the world at large.

When posting pictures from parties or gatherings, a lady makes sure she has the permission of others who appear in the pictures. Some people may feel that a picture is misleading or that it is unflattering to them and their reputation. Not everyone wants the world to witness their fun times.

A lady reviews and updates her profile to ensure that her information is current.

⌒

A lady always considers her actions carefully before posting a "crazy "action-filled video of herself. Such videos can affect a lady's professional career, her acceptance to a certain college, her membership in a sorority or club, and her personal relationships for years to come. She remembers that everything ever sent out via e-mail or on the Internet will be stored on someone's hard drive. The fact that a lady, after a change of heart, has deleted something that might cause her embarrassment does not mean that it was completely removed from cyberspace.

⌒

A lady remembers that first impressions both personal and professional, within a network setting, are lasting.

A lady always does her best to remain positive. She does not write negative comments about friends, coworkers, her employers, or her employees.

～

A lady does not send photographs of herself over the Internet to people she does not know.

～

A lady never sends photographs of herself wearing skimpy clothing—or even less— to anyone, not even her boyfriend. She realizes that not all relationships last and that such photographs might come back to haunt her one day.

～

If a lady's friends have posted photographs of her that make her even the least bit uncomfortable, she un-tags herself, and if warranted, asks them to delete them immediately.

～

A lady does not "sext."

A lady does not send text messages she would be embarrassed for others to see.

⌒

A lady is never so desperate for a man's attention that she lowers her standards or does anything she will be less than proud of later.

⌒

While it may not seem so, a lady realizes that the content of any e-mail she sends may be permanent or find its way into the hands of others and is careful not to say anything she wouldn't want others to read.

⌒

A lady always congratulates others on their advancements in professional careers.

⌒

A lady always tries to help others, offering them tips, information, guidance, or business history that she feels may be helpful to them.

A lady always puts her best foot forward and takes care to make her best appearance. She is mindful that a professional headshot on her business network profile is key. She does not use casual or party type pictures for a headshot.

The Etiquette of the Office Break Room

Even if a lady is not meticulous about how she behaves in her own kitchen, she maintains higher standards in the office break room or the communal kitchen. She never leaves her dirty coffee cup, her dirty dishes, or her dirty silverware in the sink. If there is no dishwasher, she washes her own dishes. She also dries them and puts them away.

If she takes the last of stocked items (paper towels, soda, or ice) she refills them. Likewise, if she takes the last cup of coffee, she makes a fresh pot.

She does not leave her leftovers in the office refrigerator for an excessively long time. And she never assumes that she has an automatic right to sample anything left in the refrigerator by a fellow employee.

At the office, as at home, a lady always refills the ice trays.

⌢

A lady shares her home phone number only with those business associates who really need it. She does not give out the home phone numbers of people who work with her.

⌢

A lady delivers messages she takes on behalf of someone else in an accurate and timely manner.

⌢

A lady does not barge into another person's office, even if the door has been left open.

⌢

A lady may choose to carry work home from the office or devote more time to her job than others do. She does not, however, assume that her fellow employees will do the same.

A lady knows that sick children are more important than a deadline at the office.

A lady does not miss deadlines.

When a lady recognizes an outstanding contribution of a coworker, she not only expresses her feelings with the coworker but also with her boss.

A lady remains composed at the office. Should she feel herself losing composure, whether losing her temper or on the verge of tears, she calmly excuses herself.

A lady does not play music in her office so loudly that it disturbs others.

If a lady works in a cubicle, she is careful not to speak so loudly as to disturb others around her regardless of whether she is on a business call or talking to a coworker in person.

Chapter Nine

A LADY TAKES CARE OF HERSELF

A lady sees her doctors on a regular basis, especially her gynecologist.

~

A lady knows that monthly breast self-exams are smart and life-saving no matter what age she is. She reports any irregularities to her doctor. Prevention and early detection are the best ways to beat breast cancer.

~

A lady never leaves discarded feminine hygiene products in an open wastebasket at someone else's home or at the office. She always properly wraps these items and discreetly disposes of them.

A lady knows how to defend herself and takes a self-defense course if she chooses.

❧

A lady does not hug other people after she has been working out or running unless she explains what she has been doing and her friend insists on a hug anyway.

❧

When a lady senses that she is not in a safe place, she leaves as calmly and quickly as possible.

❧

When faced with life's minor setbacks, a lady does not act like a victim.

❧

When life deals bad breaks, a lady rises above them.

A Lady and Breast Cancer

Breast cancer can occur at any age, young or old, but a lady knows it is smart to check monthly for signs of a lump, tenderness, or discoloration on any part of her breasts. She is proactive by making an appointment with her doctor if she notices an unexplained change. She knows that an early diagnosis of breast cancer can save her life as she faces the challenge of keeping herself healthy and well.

Smoking

A lady knows that smoking is harmful to her health. If she chooses to smoke, a lady is considerate about other people's air space. A lady never smokes when pregnant, knowing that it is harmful—possibly deadly—to her baby and may cause complications in her pregnancy, such as low birth weight or a premature delivery.

A lady does not smoke around children nor does she smoke around expectant mothers. She knows that secondhand smoke is harmful to children inside and outside the womb, causing asthmatic symptoms.

A lady knows the risk that smoking has on her reproductive health and weighs the risks and harmful effects before deciding to take up such a habit.

A Lady and Her Gynecologist

A lady makes yearly appointments with her doctor or gynecologist to insure that she stays healthy and aware of any problems. She is smart to make a Pap smear part of her regular checkup because she knows that her body can go through strong hormonal changes that can lead to emotional and physical distress.

A lady makes an appointment with her gynecologist if she experiences any change in her menstrual cycle—heavier or longer bleeding time, spotting in between monthly periods, or pain that is prolonged and unusual. She knows that early detection of reproductive problems can lead to cures and safeguard her from infertility.

A lady knows that she is at her best when she is in good health. And for that reason, she does not ignore her health.

~

A lady realizes that a tan is not worth the risk of skin cancer. She uses sun block when she goes out in the sun. A lady knows there are many products on the market today that will give her the appearance of a tan without the danger.

~

A lady is not ashamed to ask for the sexual history of a man with whom she may become intimate.

~

A lady does not lead men on.

~

A lady is never afraid to go to the proper authority figures to report inappropriate physical or sexual abuse.

A lady never gives her telephone number to a stranger over the Internet. If she wishes to meet someone she has chatted with, she arranges to meet him or her in a safe place.

~

A lady expects the men in her life to understand the meaning of the word "no." Otherwise, she simply does not make them a part of her life.

~

A lady has a circle of friends and family members to whom she goes for advice and counsel.

~

A lady never gets behind the wheel of her car if she has had too much to drink.

~

A lady knows that even a couple of drinks may be "too much."

A lady is cautious not to put herself in harmful situations that could endanger her safety or compromise her own personal value system for living.

⌒

If a lady doesn't see well, she wears her glasses or her contact lenses. She doesn't let vanity stand in her way of seeing all life has to offer—including traffic signals and turn signals on the road.

⌒

A lady does not just order a salad at a restaurant when she is on a date if she really wants a hamburger. She realizes the men who would not want her because she has an appetite are not worth the trouble.

A Lady Protects Herself

In a world where everyone's personal safety has been challenged—in schools, the workplace, parking lots, and even while pumping gas at a busy service station—a lady equips herself with the knowledge and skills necessary for protecting herself, should she be threatened. She reads articles, attends seminars, or takes self-defense courses to prepare herself should there ever be an unexpected assault or attack.

A lady knows that her posture and confident appearance can help deter an attacker from choosing her as his next victim. She walks with her shoulders back and her head and chin high, giving her an air of power and self-assurance to an outside observer. A lady knows that her confident body language makes her appear to be a less vulnerable or passive victim.

When a lady senses she is not in a safe place or if a person gives her cause to doubt her safety, she leaves calmly and quickly. She does not show the sense of fear that might make her more vulnerable to a threatening action or attack.

- Regardless of how prepared she is for possible attacks, a lady tries to avoid, at all costs, situations and places that may put her at risk.

- When pumping gas, a lady makes sure that no one enters her car from the passenger side.

- A lady looks underneath the car and in the back seat before getting in.

- A lady is careful not to park next to a van in a parking lot. She knows that women have been abducted from parking lots when snatched by an attacker who jumps from a van and pulls them into the vehicle.

- A lady is careful always and keeps the doors to her home and her automobile locked.

- A lady is aware of high crime areas and does not visit them alone or after dark.

- A lady does not walk through a parking lot alone if possible. She is aware of the people around her, especially anyone who may be following her.

- Ladies on cell phones and fumbling in their purses are already distracted and are easier targets for robbery or abduction.

- Women are less likely to become targets for attack if they carry an umbrella or another sharp object that they can use to protect themselves.

- A lady knows that a man's groin is his most vulnerable spot. She knows how to go for that area by kneeing an attacker, rendering him helpless, and allowing her to escape.

- Faced with an attacker, a lady is not passive. She yells! Screams! Kicks!

When a lady's car breaks down on the highway, she does not attempt to flag down a passing motorist. Instead, she uses her cell phone or waits for a law enforcement officer to arrive.

⌒

In today's world, a lady knows that, with the advent of cameras on cell phones, she is always on display.

⌒

If a lady makes a date with someone she has met online, she informs a close friend about the details.

⌒

A lady never gives her financial information online to any person or business that she has not researched.

⌒

A lady knows that if a deal, or a potential relationship, appears too good to be true, it usually is.

When a lady travels, especially in foreign countries, she is careful to keep her purse and wallet secure, so that it is less likely to tempt a pickpocket.

⌒

Before she travels, a lady makes sure her passport is up to date.

⌒

When planning a trip, a lady keeps copies of important documents, such as copies of her driver's license, passport, and credit cards, as well as her travelers' check numbers, in a separate place from the originals, in case of emergency.

⌒

A lady carries her health insurance and automobile insurance information with her at all times.

Before a lady rents a car, and before she declines the rental company's insurance policy, she makes sure that her own automobile insurance covers her in the event of an accident.

⌒

When she is in an accident, a lady calls the police, even if the other party insists they will take care of the damage without getting the police involved.

⌒

If a lady finds herself in a place or situation in which she is uncomfortable, she leaves.

⌒

A lady stands up for herself and is never a doormat.

Chapter Ten

EXTREME ETIQUETTE

At the White House

If a lady is invited to the White House, she must accept the invitation. Depending on the formality of the invitation (engraved on heavy paper, complete with the presidential seal), a lady should reply with a written formal note of acceptance. Should she receive a less formal invitation in the form of a phone call or a letter from the First Lady's assistant or the president's secretary, the lady should respond in the manner in which the invitation was issued. A formal invitation should be responded to on the most formal stationery available.

When visiting the White House, a lady dresses in her best suit or dress for daytime events or evening wear if attending an evening event.

A lady is always cautious to be moderate with her consumption of alcohol. She does not smoke at any time on the White House premises.

Realizing that the schedules of the president and his or her spouse are busy, to say the least, a lady arrives at the appointed hour and says her goodbyes at the appointed time. If she is fortunate enough to be asked to have her photograph taken with any member of the first family, she accepts and stands where she is directed, even if it is not her "best side."

And even though it is the White House, a lady promptly sends a thank-you note to express her appreciation for the time she was fortunate to spend with our country's leaders.

Meeting the President

When a lady is in a receiving line to meet the president, she addresses the president as "Mr. [or Madame] President" as the case may be or "Sir" or "Ma'am."

The president's spouse is greeted by his or her married name as in "Mrs. Cromwell" or "Mr. Cromwell."

No one in the room sits until the president and his or her spouse sits down.

A lady waits for the president to initiate a handshake and any passing conversation. Even if she does not agree with a recent action this president has taken, she does not use this time to express her displeasure.

An Audience with the Pope

When a lady visits Rome, the highlight of her visit may be an audience with the pope. Whether she is Catholic or non-Catholic, a lady will need great connections to gain an audience. Her request must be arranged through prominent Catholic laymen or a member of the Catholic clergy. When her request is granted, she will receive a ticket for an audience at a specific time at the Vatican. The Vatican official who arranges the audience can give her further information she may need about the procedures.

A lady must be careful to dress in a black or dark everyday dress with sleeves, a conservative neckline, and a modest skirt length . Her hair must be covered. Bare legs are not acceptable. In other words, hosiery of some kind is required. Dress pants are permitted.

Everyone stands as the pope enters and leaves the audience chamber. The service will consist of a brief sermon by the pope followed by a blessing. Even non-Catholics are expected to kneel and stand along with the rest of the congregation. However, they need not cross themselves. If there is time, the pope may greet the visitors individually. The pope is referred to as "Your Holiness."

A lady knows that the Vatican is not only the headquarters for the Roman Catholic Church, but it is also one of the most famous tourist attractions in the world. For that reason, a lady makes sure to allow plenty of time to arrive at the Vatican well before her audience with the pope.

Meeting Other Public Figures

A lady may find herself with the opportunity to meet a celebrity or other famous person over the course of her lifetime. It may happen while dining out, at a charity function, or at a business convention. In any case, whenever she finds herself face to face with a well-known sports, political, or entertainment figure, she should be prepared to keep her respect and adulation in check.

No matter how excited she is to meet this celebrity, she should neither force a conversation upon him or her nor ask for an autograph. Celebrities so often hear the same compliments or questions and are frequently stopped for random autographs. It is best to expect an autograph only if autographing is the celebrity's function at the event. In some instances—as at a sports banquet or a sports convention—photographs will be readily available for signing.

A lady must never interrupt a public figure while he or she is speaking with someone else and especially if the celebrity is dining with others. If a lady does find an opportune moment to speak with a celebrity, she keeps it brief. When finished, she says, "I have enjoyed meeting and talking with you. Thank you for your time."

A lady does not gush about her admiration of the public figure and never lets them know she has been a fan since she was a little girl (even if she has.) Likewise a lady never tells a celebrity that they look younger, thinner, or better than they do on television (even if they do).

Meeting Royalty

Perhaps a lady has dreamed of meeting royalty. She may even have envisioned herself becoming a princess one day. Meeting or encountering royalty, however, entails rules of etiquette that do not apply in the United States. A lady should be prepared for that special moment by being informed of a few necessary courtesies.

If a lady is in line to meet a royal, she never attempts to initiate any conversation. If spoken to, she may reply with a simple, "So nice to meet you Ma'am (or Sir)." If a hand is extended toward her, she may extend her hand for a polite shake. If the royal asks questions of the lady, she answers them briefly and articulately. She allows the royal to bring the conversation to a close.

Should a lady have the opportunity to meet the queen of England, and if she is a citizen of the United States, she does not curtsey. Instead, she simply shakes hands if a hand is extended toward her. Otherwise, when it comes to greeting royalty, the policy is hands-off.

If a lady knows there is a chance she may have an encounter with a member of a royal family she does her homework and learns something about the family's history so that she knows enough about their home and their country to carry on a polite conversation.

Other Forms of Address for Dignitaries

The Vice President

    Mr. (Madame) Vice President or Sir (Madame)

A United States Senator

    Senator _____

A Member of the House of Representatives

    Representative _____

Governor of a State

    Governor _____

An Episcopal or Roman Catholic Bishop

    Bishop _____

A Roman Catholic Archbishop

    Your Excellency

A Rabbi

    Rabbi _____

A Member of the Protestant Clergy

    Mr. _____, Mrs. _____,
    Ms. _____, or Dr. _____

EXTREMELY FORMAL MOMENTS AT THE DINNER TABLE

HOW TO USE A FINGER BOWL

Finger bowls can be a lifesaver when eating messy seafood such as crab legs or lobster or other food eaten with your hands. If a lady is presented with a finger bowl while dining at a formal dinner, it will be placed on the dessert plate, on a doily. This is usually a small glass bowl filled three quarters with water and perhaps a slice of lemon or a flower floating in the bowl of water. A lady dips only her fingertips in the bowl of water and then dries them with her napkin. Once a lady has used her finger bowl, and as dessert is being served, she moves the bowl and doily to the upper left corner of her place setting and moves her fork and spoon to the right and left of her dessert plate.

It's Sorbet . . . and It's the Middle of Dinner!

A scoop of sorbet, arriving in the middle of dinner might leave some confused about what to do . . . but not an informed lady. She simply takes a few bites to clear her palate from the heavy taste of the entrée and leaves the rest of the sorbet to be taken away. This citrus- or liqueur-flavored sorbet in a dish is not dessert and is usually followed by a salad course. Bon Apétit!

INDEX